GUINEA
PIGS

Published in Great Britain in 2018
by Wayland

Copyright © Hodder and Stoughton, 2017

Editor: Elizabeth Brent
Produced for Wayland by Dynamo
Written by Pat Jacobs

ISBN: 978 1 5263 0146 8

10 9 8 7 6 5 4 3 2 1

Wayland, an imprint of
Hachette Children's Group
Part of Hodder and Stoughton
Carmelite House
50 Victoria Embankment
London EC4Y 0DZ

An Hachette UK Company
www.hachette.co.uk
www.hachettechildrens.co.uk

Printed and bound in China

Picture acknowledgements:

iStock: p1 ksena32; p2 LuminaStock, mwpenny, Mingzhe Zhang;
p4 adogslifephoto; p6 photokdk, Aneese, cynoclub, Gemma Rose Amos;
p7 krithnarong, Farinosa, GlobalP; p8 adogslifephoto, Farinosa,
Olesya Tseytlin, cynoclub, GlobalP; p9 DevMarya, terry6970, leaf;
p11 RomeoLu, Dantyya; p12 DevMarya, JohnatAPW; p13 Ocskaymark,
Eric Isselée; p14 icarmen13, Andrzej Tokarski, 13-Smile; p15 Elena Blokhina,
eve_eve01genesis, Mr_Mozymov; p16 Mendelex_photography;
p17 eAlisa, scigelova; p19 Crisalexo, Marco Hegner, Eric Isselée; p20 Azaliya;
p21 n1kcy, Ralph Loesche, kosobu; p23 VikaRayu, p24 AnastasiaGlazneva,
Lari Huttunen; p26 ksena32; p27 Zsolt Farkas, daizuoxin, ALLEKO,
Cloud7Days, cynoclub; p28 Eric Isselée, Ramona smiers; p29 Arkhipov;
p32 GlobalP; Front cover: photokdk; Back cover: Vassiliy Vishnevskiy

Shutterstock: p7 joannawnuk; p10 marilyn barbone; p16 Dora Zett;
p18 melis; p26 ADA_photo

Alamy: p5 Juniors Bildarchiv GmbH; p17 petographer;
p19 Maximilian Weinzierl; p20 Juniors Bildarchiv GmbH;
p22 imageBROKER; p23 Petra Wegner; p25 Maximilian Weinzierl,
Juniors Bildarchiv GmbH; p26 Juniors Bildarchiv GmbH;
p27 petographer, imageBROKER

CONTENTS

YOUR GUINEA PIG
FROM HEAD TO TAIL

Spanish sailors brought guinea pigs to Europe from South America in the 16th century. At the time, they were so expensive only wealthy people could afford them. Thanks to their gentle, friendly nature, they have become popular pets around the world.

Ears: Excellent hearing helps guinea pigs to identify predators before they come into view.

Legs: Guinea pig legs aren't very strong, and break easily, so don't let your pet fall or jump from any height.

Feet: Sharp claws help wild guinea pigs to climb mountainsides and walk on difficult ground.

Eyes: Guinea pigs' large eyes are high on the sides of their head so they can see predators coming from all directions, but they can't see right in front of their nose.

Brain: Guinea pigs have a very good memory for pathways leading to food sources.

Whiskers: Sensitive whiskers help guinea pigs to find their way in the dark, and to detect food and other objects in the blind spot in front of their nose.

Teeth: Guinea pigs are rodents so their teeth grow all the time, but as they spend most of their time chewing, they normally get worn down.

Nose: Guinea pigs have a good sense of smell, and recognise their companions and owners by their scent.

GUINEA PIG FACTS

- Guinea pigs usually live for five to eight years, but a British guinea pig called Snowball died at the age of 14 years 10 months.

- The proper name for a guinea pig is a cavy. No one knows how they got their common name because they don't come from Guinea and are not related to pigs.

GUINEA PIG BREEDS

Guinea pigs are all a similar size and, although they have individual personalities, their temperament is more or less the same whatever their breed.

Abyssinian guinea pigs are easy to spot because their hair grows in swirls, which gives their coat a rough, tufty look.

American guinea pigs have short, smooth hair and come in lots of different colour combinations. Their short coats make them easy to look after.

Peruvians are one of the oldest breeds of guinea pig. They have very long hair, which grows over their face, and they need regular grooming, bathing and trimming.

Rex guinea pigs have thick, woolly hair that stands on end, drooping ears and curly whiskers. They are easy to care for and make good pets.

Shelties (or Silkies) have long, soft hair that is swept back, so it doesn't grow over the guinea pig's face. They have to be brushed and trimmed regularly.

Skinny pigs are almost hairless, which means they need a warm place to live and a high-energy diet. Their skin is very sensitive so they need soft bedding, sunscreen when outside and regular moisturising.

Teddy guinea pigs have thick, wiry hair all over their bodies, which makes them look cuddly and round. They need brushing once a week.

Texels are high-maintenance pets. Their long, curly coats need a lot of attention to stop them from tangling and getting dirty.

CHOOSING YOUR GUINEA PIG

In the wild, guinea pigs live in small groups, made up of a male, several females and their pups. They get lonely on their own, so pet guinea pigs should be kept in pairs or groups.

MALE OR FEMALE?

You should get a single-sex pair or group. Females usually live happily together, but unless males know each other well, they may fight at first while they sort out who's in charge.

LONG- OR SHORT-HAIRED?

Short-haired guinea pigs are easy to look after, but those with longer hair need daily grooming, along with regular trimming and bathing. Guinea pigs don't always enjoy this but it is essential for their well-being.

INDOOR OR OUTDOOR PET?

Guinea pigs can live indoors, but they need a quiet space because they have sensitive hearing. Outdoor piggies should have a cage in a sheltered place, with a cosy sleeping area. If it gets really cold, you may need to bring them inside.

PET CHECK ☑

Before you buy or adopt a guinea pig, make sure that:

- its teeth meet up properly
- its eyes are sparkling
- its coat is shiny
- it doesn't have sores on its feet or legs
- it walks normally

BUY OR ADOPT?

If you want a particular type of guinea pig, you may have to buy it from a breeder, but there are lots of gorgeous guineas in rescue centres that are looking for new homes. Your local animal shelter might have the perfect pair for you.

HOME COMFORTS

Guinea pig hutches should be large enough to give each animal at least one square metre of space, and they need be completely predator-proof. Animals that attack guinea pigs include foxes, rats, dogs, cats and birds of prey.

DOS AND DON'TS

- **Do** keep the cage in a sheltered spot, where guinea pigs won't get too hot or too cold.
- **Do** cover the base with newspaper to make it easy to clean.
- **Do** give your guinea pigs a chance to run around every day, either indoors or in an outside enclosure.
- **Don't** keep guinea pigs in a garage with a car because its fumes could kill them.
- **Don't** use straw as bedding because it can poke your piggies in the eye.
- **Don't** put an outside run on grass that has been treated with weed killer.

Hay makes the best bedding – and guinea pigs can nibble on it if they feel like a midnight snack.

The hutch should be raised off the ground.

UNDERSTAND YOUR PET

I can't sweat when I get hot, so please keep me in the shade.

There should be a dark area for sleeping and a light area with a wire-mesh door so your pets have fresh air.

Hutches should have solid floors because wire floors can damage guinea pigs' feet and legs.

OUT TO GRASS

Guinea pigs love to nibble fresh grass, so if you have a lawn, they will enjoy being outside in a run during the day. They'll need water and a hiding place in case they get scared.

INDOOR PLAY

An indoor run is perfect for guinea pigs in colder weather. The walls don't have to be very high because they're not great climbers. They are easily disturbed by loud noises, so they'll need a little hidey-hole in case they feel nervous.

GET TO KNOW YOUR GUINEAS

Have the hutch, food and water ready and waiting for your guinea pigs when you bring them home. They will probably be very nervous after their journey and will run for cover as soon as you put them inside the hutch.

UNDERSTAND YOUR PET

I'm very timid, so it might take me a while to get used to being picked up.

SETTLING IN

Give your new pets a week to settle in before you start to handle them. Let them get to know you during this time by feeding them some tasty treats through the wires of their cage.

MAKING FRIENDS

When you're ready to hold your guinea pig, sit down on the floor and ask an adult to put the guinea pig on your lap. Stroke it gently while you offer it a vegetable treat.

OTHER PETS

However friendly your cat or dog might be, its scent will make guinea pigs nervous, so they should be kept apart. Rabbits often bully or kick guinea pigs, and may carry a disease that affects them, so they don't make good cage-mates.

If one of a guinea pig pair dies, you may want to get a new buddy for your remaining pet. If so, you will need to introduce them slowly.

INTRODUCING TWO GUINEA PIGS

Don't put a new guinea pig straight into another's cage because the resident piggy may attack the newcomer. Instead, put them both in an enclosure that doesn't smell of either animal, with some food to distract them. Watch them carefully – they may chase each other at first, but they should soon become friends.

GUINEA PIG GRUB

A guinea pig's main food should be good-quality hay. It is similar to their diet in the wild, and chewing hay helps to stop a guinea pig's teeth from growing too long. Any leftover hay makes a soft covering for the cage floor.

UNDERSTAND YOUR PET

Don't feed me avocado, beans, rhubarb, onions, garlic, buttercups or too much lettuce.

Guinea pigs find their food by smell, so watch out – if your fingers smell of carrot, your piggy might take a bite!

Guinea pigs love:

- Fresh grass
- Dandelions
- Clover
- Fresh herbs
- Cucumber
- Carrot (not too much)
- Melon
- Apple (no seeds)
- Banana
- Strawberries

DOUBLE DIGESTION

Guinea pigs make the most of their food by eating it twice. As well as the hard droppings you see, they produce soft ones, which the guinea pig eats directly from its bottom. These soft droppings are full of protein and vitamins.

FIVE-A-DAY

Guinea pigs, like humans, are among the few animals that don't make Vitamin C in their bodies. This means that, just like us, they need to eat fresh vegetables and fruit to stay healthy. Each guinea pig should have about a cupful every day.

If you give your piggies muesli-type food, let them empty the bowl before you top it up, otherwise they'll be missing out on an important part of their diet.

NUGGETS AND PELLETS

Guinea pig nuggets and pellets contain everything your pets need, but avoid giving them rabbit nuggets because they don't contain Vitamin C. Guinea pigs pick out their favourite bits of mixed food first and will leave the pellets that are important for their health so don't refill the bowl until they have finished everything in it.

DAY-TO-DAY CARE

Guinea pigs are easy to look after compared to lots of pets, but they still need daily care. Learn to recognise their normal behaviour, so you notice straight away if something is wrong.

PICKING UP YOUR PIGGY

A wriggling guinea pig is hard to hold and may be injured if it falls, so ask an adult to carry your pet until it knows you well enough to relax. Pick it up by sliding one hand under its stomach and cup its bottom with your other hand. Hold it firmly (not tightly) against your chest, so it feels safe.

CLAW CLIPPING

Pet guinea pigs don't walk on rough ground like their wild relatives do, so their claws often grow too long. If you notice that your piggy's claws need clipping, ask an adult to do it while you distract your pet with a treat.

BATHING

Short-haired guinea pigs rarely need bathing unless they get especially dirty, but long-haired pets should be bathed about once a month. Use special guinea pig shampoo and make sure your pets are completely dry before they go outside.

GROOMING

Brush or comb your guinea pig gently from head to tail. This will help your pet to get used to being handled and it gives you a chance to check that it doesn't have any injuries. Long-haired piggies should be groomed every day.

Let your pets run free on an easy-to-clean floor. Tell your family to watch out for the piggies and keep other pets out of the room.

UNDERSTAND YOUR PET

My wild relatives are very active and, like them, I need lots of exercise too.

17

HEALTH AND SAFETY

Guinea pigs hide injuries or illness because predators target weak animals, so it's important for owners to watch for any changes in their behaviour. If a guinea pig refuses treats, something is wrong.

MANGE MITES

If your guinea pig is scratching its skin, losing hair and suddenly doesn't like being touched, it may have mange mites. These minute creatures burrow into a guinea pig's skin and cause terrible itching. This is a very painful condition that could kill your pet, so it needs to be treated straight away.

Guinea pigs should be checked regularly for ear mites, especially if they are scratching their ears.

NEUTERING

Guinea pigs are not usually neutered because this is a big operation for a little animal. Instead, guinea pigs are kept in pairs or groups of the same sex. Neutering doesn't change a guinea pig's behaviour and won't stop males fighting.

BUMBLEFOOT

Bumblefoot is a painful infection of a guinea pig's foot pad. It happens when bacteria get into wounds caused by wire cage floors or rough bedding, so look out for swellings on the bottom of your pet's feet during grooming sessions.

Wire floors can injure guinea pigs' feet and increase the risk of bumblefoot.

UNDERSTAND YOUR PET

I love to chew, so make sure any electrical cables are out of my reach when I'm indoors.

OUTDOOR DANGERS

Predators pose the biggest risk to outdoor guinea pigs. Foxes, in particular, are very determined and can tip over lightweight cages, slide open latches and chew their way into hutches. They will also burrow under runs, so never leave your pets in their run overnight.

19

GUINEA PIG BEHAVIOUR

SCENT-MARKING

Guinea pigs are territorial animals and they scent-mark their home by rubbing their chin, cheeks and bottom on everything in their cage. They may do the same in areas where they are allowed to run free, too.

Guinea pigs are creatures of habit. They don't like change and are happiest when their owners stick to the same timetable of feeding, cleaning, exercise and cuddling every day.

TAKING COVER

In the wild, guinea pigs are food for lots of predators, including birds, so they are naturally nervous in open spaces. Your pet piggies may feel uncomfortable without a roof over their heads, so they should always have a place to hide, even indoors.

POPCORNING

'Popcorning' piggies run backwards and forwards, jumping into the air and kicking their legs out. This joyful behaviour is more common in younger guinea pigs, but happy adults sometimes popcorn too.

FREEZING

When guinea pigs are startled by a strange sound, or sense danger, they often freeze to make themselves invisible to predators. They may also make a short vibrating noise to warn the rest of the group.

SLEEPING

Guinea pigs don't sleep for long periods. Instead, they take short naps throughout the day and night. Guinea pigs have an extra, transparent eyelid that allows them to sleep with their eyes open. This means they can be on the alert for predators.

UNDERSTAND YOUR PET

Please feed me at the same time every day. I may not have a watch, but I know when it's dinner time.

COMMUNICATION

Guinea pigs are chatty little creatures. They talk to each other all the time, and they'll talk to you, too, especially if they think they might get a treat.

WHEEKING

Guinea pig owners will quickly learn to recognise this special sound that guinea pigs make when they're begging for food. Opening the fridge, cutting up vegetables or rustling bags will be enough to get your piggies wheeking.

TEETH CHATTERING

When guinea pigs are about to fight, the hairs on their back stand on end, they yawn widely and their teeth chatter. This may happen if you introduce two males that don't know each other. The best way to avoid a battle is to put a towel over one of them and take him away.

UNDERSTAND YOUR PET

If I yawn, it's not because I'm tired. I'm opening my mouth to show off my sharp teeth.

PURRING AND RUMBLING

Purring and rumbling are vibrating sounds that have different meanings. A guinea pig may purr when it's being stroked, or to reassure itself in a new situation. Rumbling is a deeper sound and normally means the guinea pig is unhappy or scared.

BOSSY BEHAVIOUR

When guinea pigs meet, they want to sort out who's the boss. 'Rumblestrutting' is part of this behaviour. The guinea pig makes a rumbling sound and wiggles its hips slowly from side to side. This is often followed by the two piggies running in a circle, nose to tail, and jumping on each other's back.

TRAINING

Guinea pigs love eating and they can be trained to obey simple commands in return for a treat. Some will learn to use a litter box, too. Never punish your pet if it doesn't do as you ask, because it will learn to be scared of you.

SIT UP AND BEG

Sitting up is natural behaviour for guinea pigs, so it's quite easy to teach your pet to sit by holding a treat above its head and saying the word 'Sit!'. Once your piggy has learned the command, it will sit when you tell it to and wait for its treat.

COME, PIGGY!

You can teach your guinea pig to come when you call by saying its name each time you give it a treat. Once your pet has learned that it will get a reward when it hears its name, try calling it during indoor exercise time.

LITTER TRAINING

Place a litter tray in the corner of the cage where you find the most droppings. Put some hay in the tray and scatter a few droppings on top. Your guinea pigs may not use their tray all the time, but if most of the droppings are in the same place, cleaning the cage will be easier.

Cat litter isn't suitable for guinea pigs because it's dusty and may cause breathing problems.

JUMPING THROUGH HOOPS

Stand a hoop on the ground in front of your guinea pig and hold a treat on the other side. When your piggy steps through the hoop, give it the treat and repeat this until it has mastered the trick. Now raise the hoop two or three centimetres off the ground so your piggy has to jump through it.

FUN AND GAMES

Guinea pigs love to run about, so they'll need some exercise time in their run, or in a safe space indoors, every day. You'll have fun watching them as they chase each other around and explore.

GUINEA PIG ACTIVITY CENTRE

Make an indoor play area or outside run more fun for your piggies by adding chew toys, balls, paper bags, tents and hidey-holes made from newspaper, and tunnels made of plastic pipe or wide cardboard tubes.

Climbing is good exercise for guinea pigs, but make sure they won't injure themselves if they fall.

MAKE A MAZE

Create a maze using cardboard boxes joined together with tube tunnels. You can extend the maze every time you get another box or tube. Put one guinea pig at one end and another at the other end and see if they meet in the middle.

UNDERSTAND YOUR PET

I'm most active in the early mornings and early evenings, so that's the best time to let me out for a run.

FIND THE FOOD

Hide your pets' favourite treats inside a cardboard tube stuffed with hay, or a screwed-up ball of paper, and watch your piggies trying to get at them.

GUINEA PIG QUIZ

How much do you know about your guinea pig pal? Try this quiz to find out.

1 Which part of the world do guinea pigs come from?

a. Australia
b. South America
c. Spain

2 Which of these is another name for a guinea pig?

a. Cavy
b. Capybara
c. Coati

3 Why shouldn't you use straw as bedding?

a. It's very expensive
b. It's poisonous for guinea pigs
c. It may poke guinea pigs in the eye

4 Which of these guinea pig breeds has long, curly hair?

a. Teddy
b. Abyssinian
c. Texel

5 What is bumblefoot?

a. A dance guinea pigs perform when they first meet
b. A painful foot infection
c. A breed of guinea pig

6 Why don't rabbits make good cage mates for guinea pigs?

a. They can pass on a disease to guinea pigs
b. They may kick and bully them
c. Both of these

10 How often should you groom a long-haired guinea pig?

a. Every day
b. Every week
c. Every month

7 Which of these foods is bad for guinea pigs?

a. Cucumber
b. Avocado
c. Apple

8 What is 'popcorning'?

a. Hiding from predators
b. Calling for food
c. Jumping in the air

9 When are guinea pigs most active?

a. At night
b. Early morning and early evening
c. At lunchtime

QUIZ ANSWERS

1 Which part of the world do guinea pigs come from?

c. South America

2 Which of these is another name for a guinea pig?

a. Cavy

3 Why shouldn't you use straw as bedding?

c. It may poke guinea pigs in the eye

4 Which of these guinea pig breeds has long, curly hair?

c. Texel

5 What is bumblefoot?

b. A painful foot infection

6 Why don't rabbits make good cage mates for guinea pigs?

c. Both of these

7 Which of these foods is bad for guinea pigs?

b. Avocado

8 What is 'popcorning'?

c. Jumping in the air

9 When are guinea pigs most active?

b. Early morning and early evening

10 How often should you groom a long-haired guinea pig?

a. Every day

GLOSSARY

bacteria – Microscopic living things, such as germs, that can cause disease.

blind spot – An area that an animal cannot see. Animals with eyes high on the sides of their head cannot see in front of their nose.

breed – All members of a breed will look more or less the same. Named guinea pig breeds have special features, such as a particular type of fur.

breeder – A person who raises particular breeds of animals.

foot pad – The soft part underneath an animal's paw.

grooming – Brushing a guinea pig's coat to keep it in good condition.

hay – Dried grass.

litter tray – A shallow tray filled with absorbant material where an animal can go to the toilet. There are special trays for small animals that fit into the corner of a cage.

mange – A skin disease caused by mites that leads to extreme itching, crusted skin and hair loss. It can kill animals if it isn't treated.

mite – A tiny creature related to a spider. Guinea pigs may suffer from ear or fur mites.

neutering – An operation that stops guinea pigs having pups. Neutering is not recommended for guinea pigs because of the risk to their health, so males and females are normally separated instead.

nuggets – Biscuit-like pellets, made from cereals and hay. They contain fibre and all the vitamins and minerals that a guinea pig needs.

predator – An animal that hunts and eats other creatures.

rodent – Rodents are animals that have to gnaw because their teeth grow throughout their life.

scent-marking – Guinea pigs use scent glands under their chin, on their cheeks and on their bottom to mark their territory and members of their family. They will usually scent-mark their cage after it's been cleaned to make it smell like home.

straw – The stems of cereal plants, such as wheat. Straw is not as soft as hay and it doesn't contain as many nutrients.

temperament – The way an animal behaves. Most guinea pigs have a gentle and friendly temperament.

territorial behaviour – When guinea pigs defend their territory they chase the intruder and try to jump onto its back to show who's in charge. Guinea pigs that look as if they might fight should be separated immediately. A guinea pig bite is very serious so protect your hands.

Vitamin C – This vitamin is found in fruit and vegetables. It protects guinea pigs (and us) from disease.

INDEX